Math in the FOREST

Rourke
Educational Media

A Division of
Carson Dellosa
Education

Elise Craver

BEFORE AND DURING READING ACTIVITIES

Before Reading: *Building Background Knowledge and Vocabulary*

Building background knowledge can help children process new information and build upon what they already know. Before reading a book, it is important to tap into what children already know about the topic. This will help them develop their vocabulary and increase their reading comprehension.

Questions and Activities to Build Background Knowledge:

1. Look at the front cover of the book and read the title. What do you think this book will be about?
2. What do you already know about this topic?
3. Take a book walk and skim the pages. Look at the table of contents, photographs, captions, and bold words. Did these text features give you any information or predictions about what you will read in this book?

Vocabulary: *Vocabulary Is Key to Reading Comprehension*

Use the following directions to prompt a conversation about each word.
*   Read the vocabulary words.
*   What comes to mind when you see each word?
*   What do you think each word means?

Vocabulary Words:
*   *compare*
*   *lines*
*   *number sentence*
*   *sets*

During Reading: *Reading for Meaning and Understanding*

To achieve deep comprehension of a book, children are encouraged to use close reading strategies. During reading, it is important to have children stop and make connections. These connections result in deeper analysis and understanding of a book.

 Close Reading a Text

During reading, have children stop and talk about the following:
*   Any confusing parts
*   Any unknown words
*   Text to text, text to self, text to world connections
*   The main idea in each chapter or heading

Encourage children to use context clues to determine the meaning of any unknown words. These strategies will help children learn to analyze the text more thoroughly as they read.

When you are finished reading this book, turn to the last page for an **After Reading Activity**.

Table of Contents

Math Is All Around 4

Numbers in the Forest 6

Measuring in the Forest 14

Shapes in the Forest 18

Photo Glossary .22

Activity 23

Index 24

After Reading Activity 24

About the Author .24

Math Is All Around

Take a walk through a forest.

Do you see math all around you?

Look up.

How tall are those trees?

How many are there?

What shapes are the trunks making?

Numbers in the Forest

Butterflies gather nectar from flowers.

How many butterflies do you see?

How can you sort them into groups?

These birds look hungry. Sort the birds into two groups.

Which group has more?

These birds are hungry too. Look at the birds on the branch and in the nest. Which has more? Take a guess.

How can you check your guess?

There are five acorns on this branch.

Three acorns on the bottom plus two acorns on the top make five acorns.

Can you make another **number sentence?**

What if some fell off the branch?

Some pine cones are in the tree.
Some have fallen on the ground.

Some are on this branch.

How would you add these three **sets** together?

Measuring in the Forest

If you are quiet, you will see animals too. Some are big, like these moose!

Some are small, like this ant.

What words could you use to **compare** these animals?

Shh! A mother bear and two cubs are walking by.

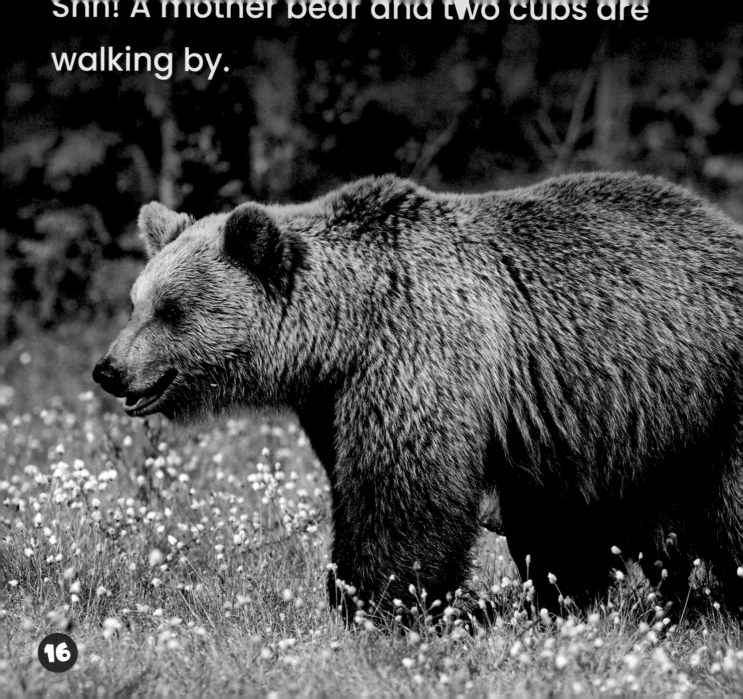

Shapes in the Forest

Hiking can be fun, but pay attention to the signs!

Use a compass to help find your way.

What shapes do you notice in this forest?

These tree trunks make tall and straight **lines**.

Look closely at the stump!

Cut a trunk open and what do you see?

Photo Glossary

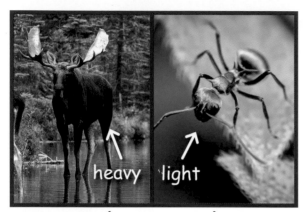

compare (kuhm-PAIR): To find what is the same and different about two groups or objects.

lines (linez): Straight geometric figures that do not bend; they go on forever in both directions.

number sentence (NUHM-bur SEN-tuhns): A true math statement that uses numbers and symbols to show how numbers are related.

sets (sets): Groups of similar objects found by sorting or grouping.

Activity: Leaf It to Me!

Leaves have different shapes, sizes, and colors. Can you sort in different ways to make counting and adding them easier?

Supplies

scissors

paper bag

wax paper (optional)

heavy book (optional)

glue

construction paper

crayons or markers

paper and pencil

Directions

1. With an adult, find some nearby trees and bushes that have leaves you can cut. If you can, go on a nature walk in a forest nearby to find the leaves. If you cannot find different leaves to cut, print pictures from the internet.

2. Use the scissors to carefully clip several sets of leaves from the branches. Collect them in your paper bag.

3. If time allows, press and dry the leaves. Place each leaf or set of leaves between two sheets of wax paper. Then, place it between the pages of a heavy book. Leave it alone for one to two weeks.

4. Carefully glue the leaves to construction paper to create a forest scene. Complete the scene with crayons or markers.

5. On another sheet of paper, write math problems you can make with the groups of leaves. Glue it to the bottom of the scene and share your work.

Index

animals 14, 15

birds 8, 9

heights 17

hiking 18

pine cones 12

tree(s) 4, 12, 20

About the Author

Elise Craver is a former teacher who lives in North Carolina. She loves to go hiking and explore all of the forests and state parks in her state. She didn't like math as a kid but loves it now. She and her two kids are always looking for math problems in real life.

After Reading Activity

Think about visiting a forest. What plants and animals do you see? Write a short story about a trip through the forest. Be sure to include the math you see along the way!

Caution: *Before beginning any nature activity, discuss any plant and animal allergies. Remind children not to touch potentially harmful plants during the activity.*

Library of Congress PCN Data

Math in the Forest / Elise Craver
(Math on My Path)
ISBN 978-1-73163-838-0 (hard cover)(alk. paper)
ISBN 978-1-73163-915-8 (soft cover)
ISBN 978-1-73163-992-9 (e-Book)
ISBN 978-1-73164-069-7 (ePub)
Library of Congress Control Number: 2020930265

Rourke Educational Media
Printed in the United States of America
02-1652111937

Edited by: Hailey Scragg
Cover design by: Rhea Magaro-Wallace, Lynne Schwaner
Interior design by: Kathy Walsh, Alison Tracey
Photo Credits: Cover, p 1 ©Filkina Natalia; p 4, 5 ©Stewart Watson; p 6, 7 ©DebraLee Wiseberg; p 8 ©Charlie Bishop; p 9 ©James Pintar; p 10, 11, 22 ©Janusz Lukomski-Prajzner; p 12, 22 ©hobo_018; p 12, 22 ©Straitel; p 13, 22 ©frederikloewer; p 14, 22 ©KeithSzafranski; p 15, 22 ©Nopphinan; p 16, 17 ©LuCaAr; p 18 ©milehightraveler; p 19 ©Smitt; p 20, 22 ©LeManna; p 21 ©LUHUANFENG; p 21 onlyyouqj